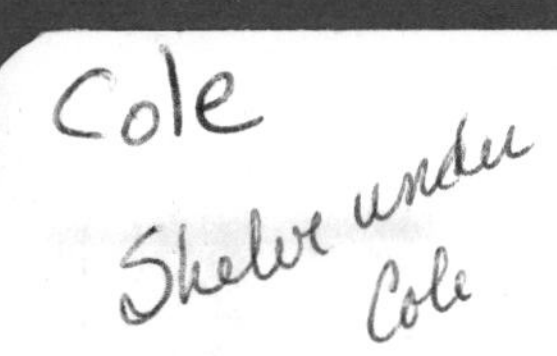

Scholastic's

The Magic School Bus®

In the Rain Forest

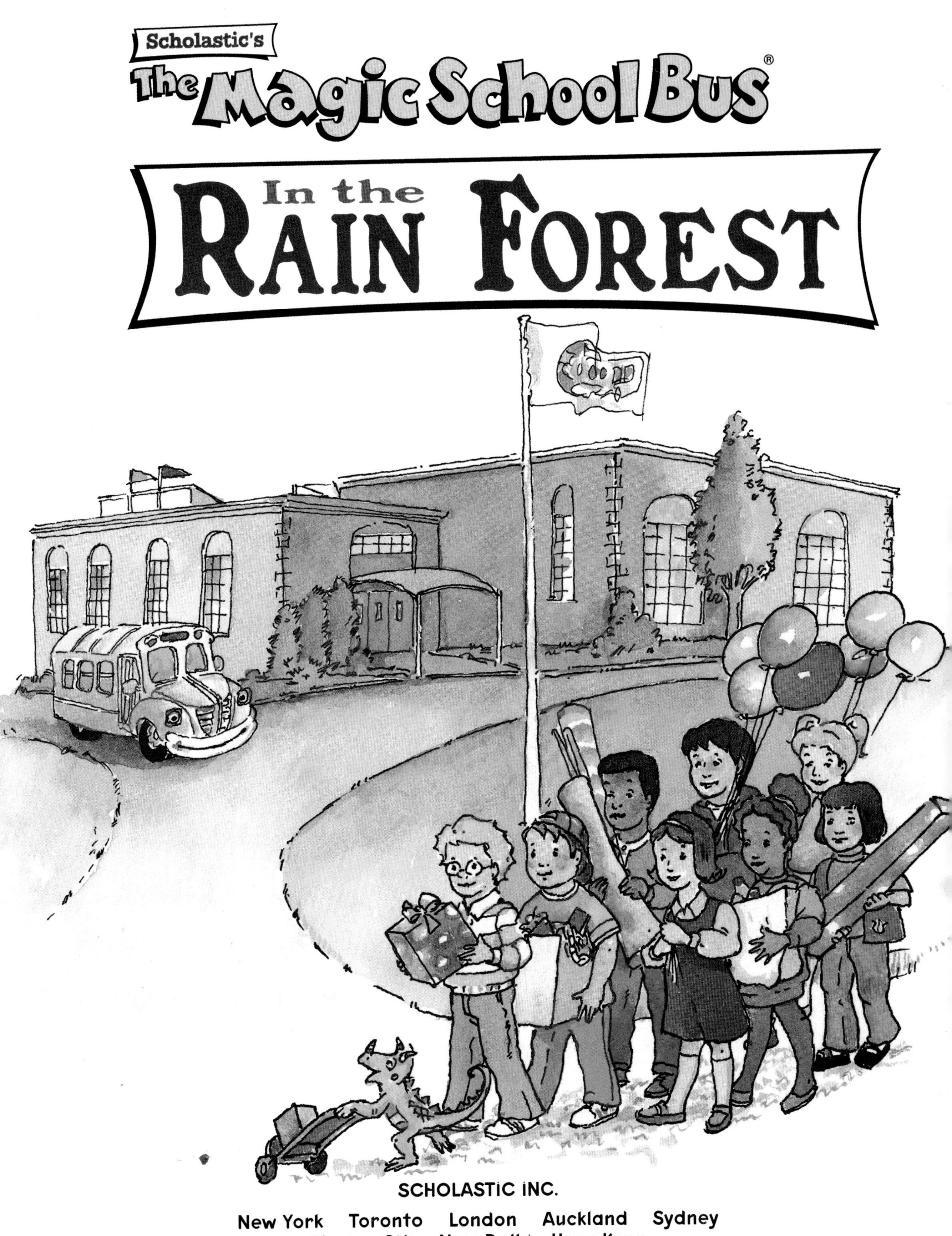

SCHOLASTIC INC.

New York Toronto London Auckland Sydney
Mexico City New Delhi Hong Kong

Based on *The Magic School Bus* books written by Joanna Cole and illustrated by Bruce Degen.

ISBN 0-590-81837-6

12 11 10 9 8 7 6 5 4 3 2 1 8 9/9 0 1 2/0

Illustrated by John Speirs
Designed by Joan Ferrigno

Also look for the Microsoft CD-ROM:
Scholastic's *The Magic School Bus Explores the Rainforest*

Printed in the U.S.A. 14

First Scholastic printing, November 1998

Our teacher, Ms. Frizzle, is full of surprises.
But on her birthday, we wanted to surprise her for a change.
We chipped in and bought her some special birthday presents.

HAPPY BIRTHDAY, MS. FRIZZLE!
All these wonderful gifts have one thing in common.
They do?

The Friz had opened up almost all her gifts. There was just one box left. She picked it up and shook it.

"It's from my great-uncle Fudge," Ms. Frizzle said. "He's president of the Choco-Bite Chocolate Factory. Strange . . . For my birthday he usually sends me a large shipment of cocoa beans from my cocoa tree in the rain forest."

When Ms. Frizzle opened the box, she found a note and one shriveled-up cocoa bean. She read the note:

DEAR NIECE,

I'M SORRY FOR THE POOR CROP THIS YEAR. FOR SOME REASON, YOUR COCOA TREE IS EXPERIENCING A COCOA BEAN SHORTAGE. HAPPY BIRTHDAY ANYWAY.

YOUR GREAT-UNCLE FUDGE

The Importance of Cocoa Beans
by Arnold
Cocoa beans are one of the most important crops in the world because they are used to make chocolate!

How to Make Chocolate

In a tropical rain forest cocoa seeds, or beans, grow inside pods.

Workers cut off the ripe pods and scoop out the beans.

The beans are covered (fermenting stage) and left to rest for 7 to 10 days. Then they are dried and shipped to the chocolate factory.

At the factory, the beans are cleaned and ground into a substance called chocolate liquor. All chocolate products are made from chocolate liquor.

WHAT IS A TROPICAL RAIN FOREST?
A tropical rain forest is a forest where it's wet and warm all year round. The rain and heat help many kinds of trees and plants grow fast. The trees and plants make good homes for zillions of animals.
That's what Ms. Frizzle meant.
All these gifts come from the rain forest!

"Why isn't your cocoa tree making beans?" Tim asked.

Ms. Frizzle's eyes lit up. "A reasonable question, Tim!" she said. She headed for the door. "And I know where we can find the answer. Everybody to the bus! Next stop — a tropical rain forest!"

GIFTS FROM THE RAIN FOREST
Many of our favorite foods and plants were first discovered in rain forests. Rain forest plants are used to make such products as skin lotion, herbal tea, and life-saving drugs.

The next minute, we were aboard the Magic School Blimpbus, on our way to find Ms. Frizzle's cocoa tree.

"Whoa!" said Carlos as we floated above the rain forest. "It's wall-to-wall trees down there!"

"The treetops are so close together that it looks like they're connected to each other," Phoebe said.

Keesha was worried. "How are we ever going to find Ms. Frizzle's tree?"

Where Are the Tropical Rain Forests?
by Wanda
Tropical rain forests are all near the earth's equator, where the weather is always warm.

What is the Equator?
by Phoebe
The equator is an imaginary line around the earth's middle.

Ms. Frizzle gave us waterproof ponchos to put on and handed us each an umbrella.

"There's one thing you can count on in a rain forest," she said. "It's rain!"

Liz opened a hatch in the bottom of the blimpbus.

Ms. Frizzle counted to three, and we jumped!

There's No Place on Earth Like a Rain Forest
by Arnold

Rain forests cover only a small part of Earth, but *half* of all kinds of plants and animals live there!

In my old school, we never jumped out of blimps.

I hope there aren't any holes in this umbrella!

The Green Roof/Part I
by Keesha
The tallest trees form a roof over the rain forest floor. This level of the rain forest is called the canopy.

Down, down we floated.

"Look at all the different kinds of trees!" Phoebe said.

"And insects!" cried Wanda.

"And birds," Arnold pointed out.

According to my research, the rain forest has more than 1,500 kinds of butterflies.

SEEN ONLY IN THE RAIN FOREST

300 different kinds of trees in an area the size of two football fields!

50 different kinds of ants and 1,000 different kinds of beetles in a space the size of a two-car garage!

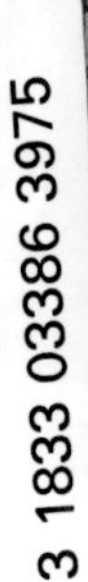

Tim landed on the branch of a leafy, fruit-filled tree. He saw a strange plant sitting on the branch.

"Wow!" he called. "There's a whole little world right inside this plant!"

"Right you are, Tim!" the Friz called as she floated past.

"That plant is called a bromeliad. These plants are named after a scientist from Sweden, Olaf Bromelius, who first discovered them."

Olaf Bromelius's Great Discovery
by Tim

A bromeliad doesn't need soil — it grows right on a tree.

A tight ring of leaves on top of the plant catches rainwater and makes a little pond. Dozens of small animals and plants live in the pond.

The Green Roof/Part II
by Keesha

More animals live in the canopy than in any other part of the rain forest. Many spend their whole lives in the tree-tops. They never touch ground at all!

Orchids!

As we floated down to the level below the canopy, the forest grew darker, but there were still bright patches of sunlight.

Hummingbirds!

Bats!

Ants!

A Feast for Anteaters
by Wanda
One rain forest in Central America has 135 kinds of ants. For an anteater, that's a different ant meal every day for 4 1/2 months!

Boas!

Tree frogs!

A Note from D.A.
The trees below the canopy are called the understory.

Ocelots!

Look for this tree.

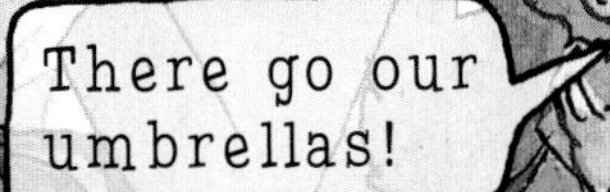

This place is crawling with creatures!

Finally, we were on the forest floor. Somewhere down here was Ms. Frizzle's cocoa tree. But where?

Life in the Leaf Litter
by Carlos
Fallen leaves make a layer of soil called the leaf litter. All kinds of bugs and animals live in the leaf litter — even snakes and scorpions.

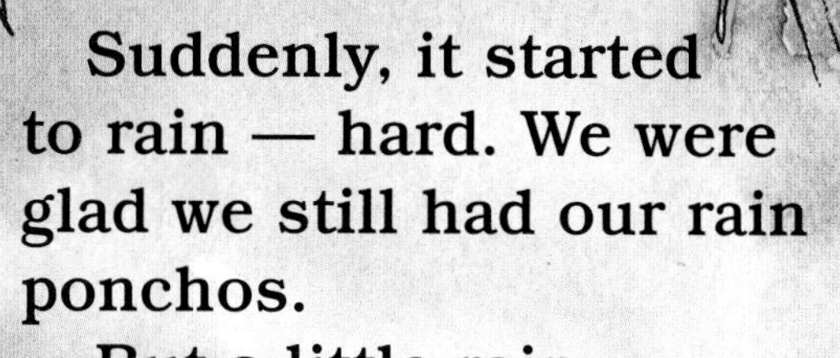

Suddenly, it started to rain — hard. We were glad we still had our rain ponchos.

But a little rain wouldn't stop us from finding Ms. Frizzle's tree.

Wet, Wetter, Wettest
by Arnold

A rain forest has two seasons—wet and not so wet. About 6 1/2 feet of rain falls each year. Some places get more than 18 feet! It rains hard for a short time almost every day. Then the sun comes out again.

COMPARISON

Rain Forest
Louisiana
Nevada

What is the wettest part of the U.S.?

Louisiana gets almost 4 1/2 feet of rain a year.

They should send some to Nevada. It only gets 9 inches a year.

These other trees don't have pods, either!
My tree!
This cocoa tree should have pods.

The Truth about Cocoa Trees
by Carlos
Pods are the fruit of the cocoa tree. Many trees grow their leaves and flowers before their fruit. Cocoa trees are different. They have leaves, flowers, and fruit all the time.

The rain stopped just as we came to a patch of trees that was surrounded by a fence.

"These are cocoa trees!" Ms. Frizzle said.

"Why did someone put a fence around them?" Ralphie asked.

We went through the gate. Ms. Frizzle's tree was right in the middle of the patch. It had lots of flowers, but no pods.

Fruit Facts
Fruits contain seeds.
These are all fruits.

A man in a white suit and hat came running up.

"Stop! Stop!" he called. "I am Inspector Number 47 of the Choco-Bite Chocolate Factory, and you are trespassing on my patch of cocoa trees."

"Is that so?" Dorothy Ann said. "Well, this tree belongs to Ms. Frizzle. And we would like to know why it doesn't have any pods."

The man shook his head. "It's a mystery. I think that Inspector 46 has been messing around with my trees. He is jealous of my clean, mud-free zone. Thanks to my fence, you will not find any pesky peccaries making mud wallows on my land. No nasty bugs, either! Soon I will get promoted over him. Someday I may even be Inspector Number 1!

"And now it is time for my lunch," the inspector said as he walked off. "Don't forget to close the gate when you leave."

What are peccaries?
They are small wild pigs.
We may be in for a wild time.

"I'll bet there's another reason the trees have stopped making pods," Wanda said.

Just then we saw a hummingbird flying from one orchid flower to another with pollen on its beak.

We knew that flowers need to be pollinated in order to grow into seeds and fruit — such as cocoa beans and pods.

"Pollen!" Tim cried. "Maybe Ms. Frizzle's tree didn't get pollinated."

A Note from D.A.
Pollinate means to carry pollen from one flower to another.

This may be a case of missing pollen!

But Ms. Frizzle's flowers had plenty of pollen.

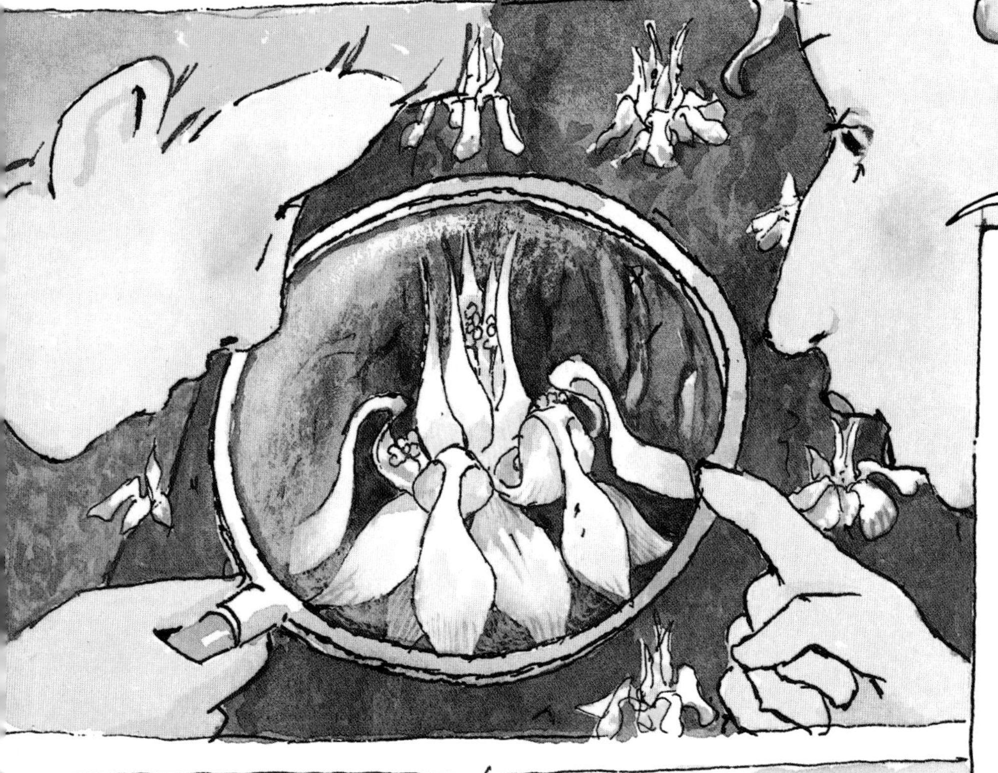
Pollen has to travel for its secret to unravel.

Chief Pollinators of the Rain Forest
Birds
Bats
Insects

"Watch out!" cried Arnold. "Here comes a bee. I think it's going to pollinate Ms. Frizzle's tree!"

"No way, Arn," D.A. said. "The bee is too big to get into a cocoa tree flower."

"There must be some really tiny insects to carry pollen between cocoa flowers," Tim said. "But where are they?"

This may be a case of missing insects!
We'll find them. To the bus!

Our bus was back just in time to help us look for the tiny insects that could pollinate Ms. Frizzle's cocoa tree.

As we left Inspector 47's cocoa patch, we heard a message over a loudspeaker:

"You are now leaving the mud-free zone. Beware of the peccaries, the bugs, and the filthy mud!"

"Boy," Wanda said, "Inspector 47 sure hates mud."

A connection worth detection, Tim!

I bet the mud-free zone has something to do with the missing cocoa beans.

PECCARIES MAKE DITCHES
When peccaries wallow in the mud to cool off, they make ditches. Rain fills up the ditches to make little drinking pools.

PECCARIES POKE AROUND
Peccaries root in the forest leaf litter to find food — fruit, seeds, plants, and small snakes.

"Look out! Peccaries ahead!" D.A. called out suddenly.

Ms. Frizzle slammed on the brakes, and the bus went skidding through the mud. The peccaries ran off into the forest, followed by some black-and-white birds and lots of little bugs.

NUNBIRDS FOLLOW PECCARIES

The birds eat the insects that fly out of the leaf litter when peccaries look for food.

We got out of the bus to look around — and found ourselves ankle-deep in a mud wallow!

"Welcome to Mudville," D.A. said.

"You mean Bugville," Tim said, swatting at the insects that were swarming around us.

"This bug happens to go by the name of midge fly, Tim," Ms. Frizzle informed him.

Suddenly, we heard Keesha calling out.

"Look, everybody! All these cocoa trees are filled with pods!"

The cocoa trees were right next to the peccaries' mud wallow. We could see midge flies around the flowers.

Tim had an idea. “Quick, D.A., give me that magnifying glass.” Tim stared through the magnifying glass at an insect in the mud.

“It seems that a watery mud wallow is a perfect place for laying eggs and raising baby midge flies. In short, a mud wallow for peccaries is also home sweet home for midge flies.”

I get it! Midge flies carry the pollen . . .
. . . from one cocoa flower to the next.
And the pollinated flowers grow into pods . . .

. . . that are filled
with cocoa beans . . .

. . . that are used
to make chocolate!

Now we knew what had happened to Ms. Frizzle's tree.

"We must inform the inspector instantly!" the Friz announced. "All aboard the bus!"

Inspector 47 was back from lunch.

Dorothy Ann held up a glass jar with midge flies inside. "This is what your cocoa trees need, Mr. Inspector. Without midge flies, the flowers cannot get pollinated and make pods."

"And midge flies cannot be born without the mud wallows the peccaries make!" Tim said.

"Mud? Peccaries? Oh dear, oh dear!" The inspector's face turned red. "You mean the trees need these animals in order to grow beans? What have I done? Now I will never get promoted!"

"Don't be so sad," Phoebe said. "We can repair the link between the peccaries and cocoa beans by returning things to the way they were — can't we?"

The inspector snapped his fingers. "Yes!" he cried. "The fence will come down tomorrow!"

"Uh-oh," Tim said. "We may not have to wait until tomorrow. I think I hear the pounding of peccary hooves coming this way right now."

Just as the peccaries came running into the mud-free zone, it started to pour.

The dried mud wallows filled with water, and the peccaries rolled around in the fresh mud.

It's raining again?
It is a rain forest.

When the rain stopped, the hot, humid air was filled with the buzz of midge flies.

"Hurray!" the inspector cried. "The midge flies are back. Now my trees will grow lots of beans again. I'll get a promotion after all!"

"Good luck!" we called as we climbed back into the bus pickup. Ms. Frizzle pulled a lever and the pickup whirled itself into the flying blimpbus. We were on our way home.

When we got back home, Ms. Frizzle told us some bad news about the rain forests of the world — they are disappearing!

That's because rain forests are being burned or cut down to make room for new villages and farms, and to get wood for fuel or to make furniture and paper products.

Every year there is less rain forest than there was the year before.

All over the world, people are trying to find ways to stop the destruction before it's too late.

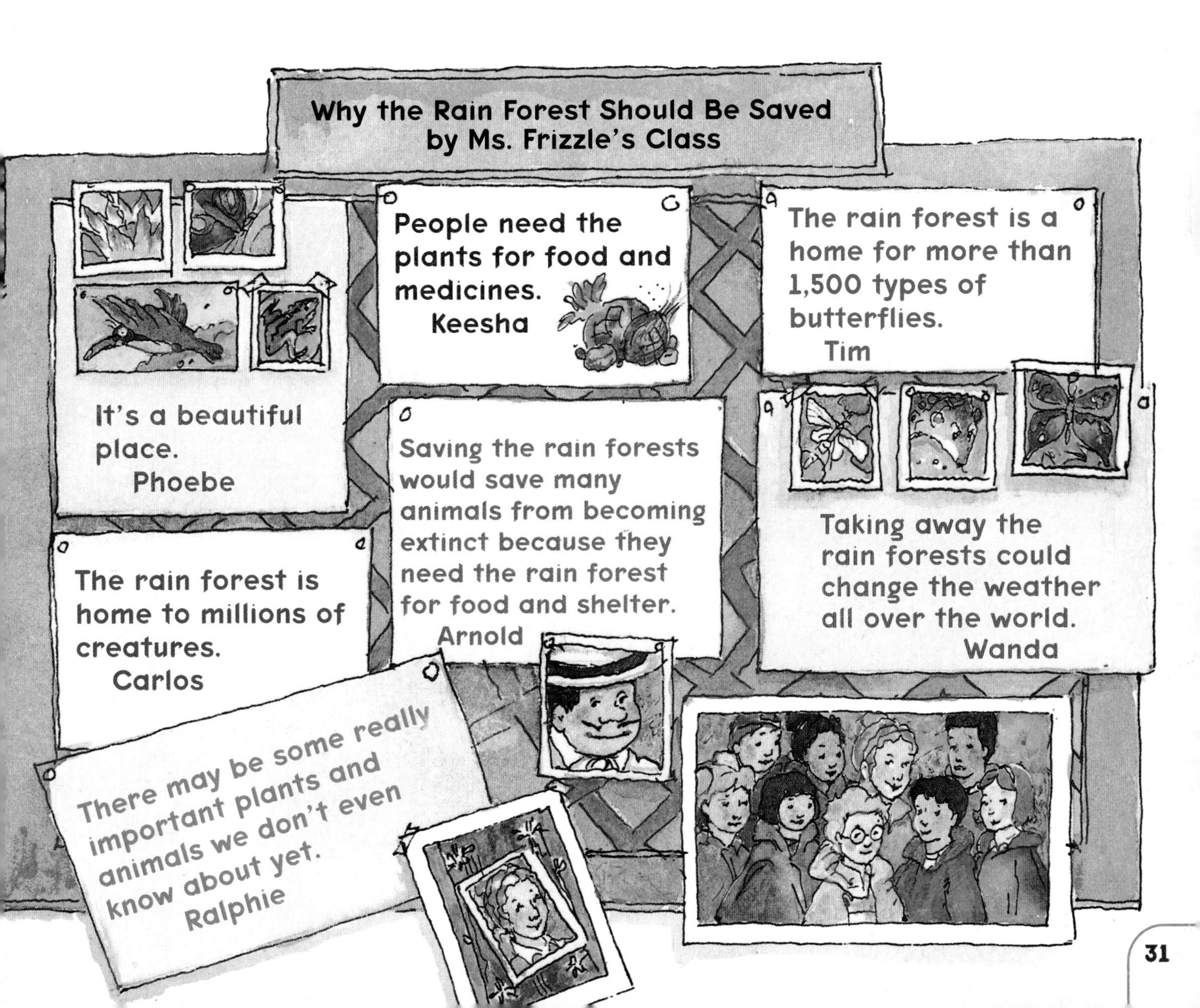

Why the Rain Forest Should Be Saved
by Ms. Frizzle's Class
It's a beautiful place.
Phoebe
People need the plants for food and medicines.
Keesha
The rain forest is a home for more than 1,500 types of butterflies.
Tim
The rain forest is home to millions of creatures.
Carlos
Saving the rain forests would save many animals from becoming extinct because they need the rain forest for food and shelter.
Arnold
Taking away the rain forests could change the weather all over the world.
Wanda
There may be some really important plants and animals we don't even know about yet.
Ralphie

A few months later, Ms. Frizzle got another delivery from the Choco-Bite Chocolate Factory. There was a note.

"It's from the inspector!" Ms. Frizzle said. She read the note to us:

I AM HAPPY TO REPORT THAT YOUR TREE IS DOING VERY WELL NOW. A FULL SHIPMENT OF COCOA BEANS IS ON ITS WAY.

VERY TRULY YOURS,

INSPECTOR 22.

P.S. THANKS TO YOU, I GOT A BIG PROMOTION!